WHO WAS

Aethelflaed

- Aethelflaed was the daughter of Alfred the Great, King of Wessex. Her mother was Ealhswith, a Mercian noble lady; Aethelflaed had a younger brother, Edward, who became known as Edward the Elder.

- She was probably born in 869 at Chippenham, in Wessex but close to the border with Mercia.

- Around 886 Aethelflaed marries Aethelred, the Lord of the Mercians and a friend of Alfred.

- After 901 little is heard of Aethelred, until his death in 911; he may have become ill or was wounded in battle.

- After 901 Aethelflaed appears to be the ruler of the Mercians and becomes known as the Lady of the Mercians. In Wales she is called Queen of the Mercians but she never gives herself this title.

- From the age of 6 Athelstan, Edward's son, is brought up by Aethelflaed in Mercia.

To Alison

David Guest

J.S. Guest.

WHO WERE THE VIKINGS

Vikings were raiding armies that came to Britain across the North Sea from Denmark (Danes) and Norway (Norse).

CHIPPENHAM

When she was no more than 8 or 9 years old, Aethelflaed was enjoying Christmas with her family at the town of Chippenham, a royal stronghold. Not far away, at Gloucester, a Viking army led by King Guthrum had made camp for the winter in the old Roman town. The Vikings usually waited for the warm spring sunshine before going out on their raids so Aethelflaed and her family felt quite safe to enjoy their Christmas festivities. Unfortunately Guthrum, not being a Christian, had decided not to play by the normal rules and suddenly appeared outside the town walls of Chippenham and was very soon inside. It was rumoured that Guthrum had been helped by a treacherous Anglo-Saxon who had fallen out with Alfred.

Whatever the truth, it was Guthrum and his friends who enjoyed the comforts of Chippenham while Aethelflaed and her family were driven out into the cold winter night. But at least they were alive, many of their friends may not have been so lucky.

ATHELNEY

While there were other royal towns which would probably have been more comfortable, Alfred took his family to Athelney, an island fortress rising up from the swamps and marshes of an area called the Somerset Levels. Here Alfred felt safe from attack and could plan his next move.

King Alfred

THE BATTLE OF EDINGTON

By the spring Guthrum and his friends were starting to run short of food so they decided to do what Vikings enjoyed doing most - go on a raid.

Perhaps the Vikings now had a traitor in their army, or perhaps Alfred just had very good spies, because he seemed to know exactly what Guthrum was up to. Alfred sent messengers to order all the men of Somerset, Wiltshire and Hampshire to meet at Egbert's Stone. Egbert was a famous Wessex King and this stone was presumably erected in his honour on Salisbury Plain: it was on an ancient trackway and would have been well known to local people thereby making it easy to find.

Once they had gathered, Alfred marched his men across Salisbury Plain, making sure they weren't spotted by any Vikings. Aethelflaed and the rest of the families marched with them. It was their job to look after the fighting men – this was the role of Wessex women. Alfred, however, was a strong believer in education and Aethelflaed was a good learner and all the time she was learning how to defeat a raiding Viking army.

Eventually, Alfred attacked and defeated Guthrum at Edington, a village below the edge of Salisbury Plain. The Vikings retreated back to Chippenham without having found any food. Alfred blockaded the town until, with their stomachs rumbling, the Vikings were forced to surrender.

Guthrum

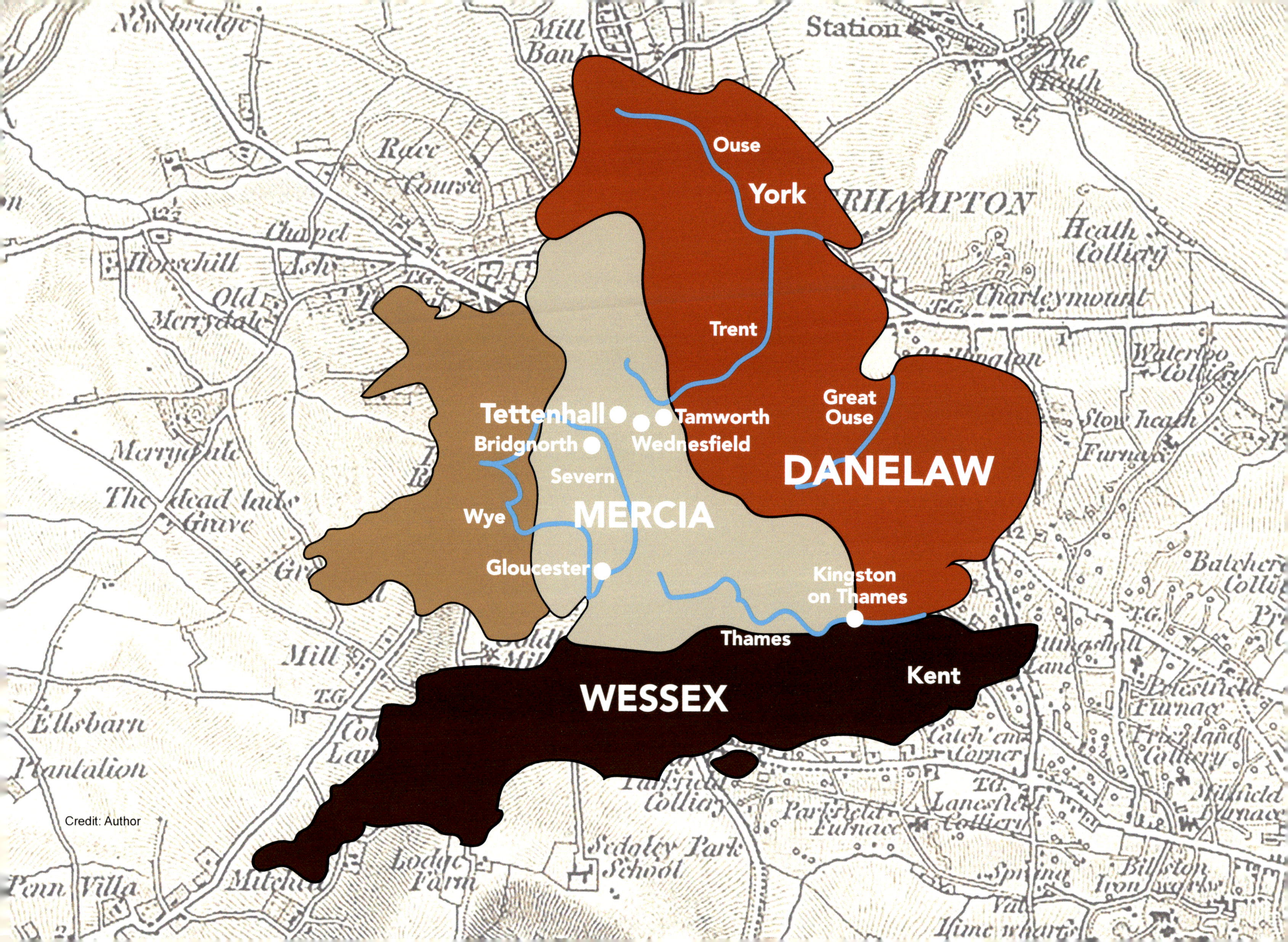

Ouse

York

Trent

Great
Ouse

Tettenhall

Bridgnorth

Severn

Tamworth

Wednesfield

DANELAW

Wye

MERCIA

Gloucester

Kingston
on Thames

Thames

Kent

WESSEX

BRITAIN DIVIDED

After all that had happened at Chippenham it must have been very satisfying for Aethelflaed to see the mighty Viking leader, Guthrum, grovel before her father. But what would Alfred do? Aethelflaed watched and learnt how to negotiate with these Vikings.

First of all Guthrum had to promise to be a good Christian and he was baptised and given a new name, Athelstan. He then had to promise to stop raiding Anglo-Saxon lands. In return the Vikings could rule over all of Britain east of the Roman Watling Street – the area which came to be known as the Danelaw. Not a bad deal as the alternative was probably to be executed on the spot!

There were, however, two problems. The first was that Viking leaders were not well known for keeping promises so Alfred took some of Guthrum's friends as hostages and they would certainly have been executed if he broke his promise.

The second problem was that Guthrum was the leader of only one Viking army: there were plenty of others who had not made any promises to Alfred. There would be much to do if Aethelflaed was to protect her Anglo-Saxon people in the future.

THE LADY OF THE MERCIANS

After 901, with her husband ill or wounded, it is Aethelflaed's responsibility to look after and protect the people of Mercia. Learning again from her father she begins building fortified towns called burhs making use of old stone age camps or dilapidated Roman forts such as at Worcester, Gloucester and Chester. She also built new burhs at places such as Shrewsbury and Bridgnorth, which grew into the towns that exist today. In each of these towns, men lived and worked with their families, but at times of danger these men could be quickly called upon to fight any Viking raiders.

CHESTER

In 907 a Viking tribe was thrown out of Ireland by an Irish king and were looking for somewhere to settle. They asked Aethelflaed if they could have land near Chester. As there was probably plenty of land available, Aethelflaed agreed – as long as they kept out of Chester itself. At first the Vikings kept to the bargain, but soon they decided to try and seize the old Roman town. Rather than fight a battle outside the town, which would have meant that many of her subjects would be killed in battle, Aethelflaed ordered everyone back inside the town walls. It is then said that an Irishman in the Viking army let it be known that there was one gate that would be left open where the Vikings could easily sneak in at night. It was a trap. The gate was suddenly forced shut trapping half the Viking army inside the walls and at the mercy of the Mercian defenders. Naturally the Vikings left outside the walls were not happy about this and laid siege to the town. According to an Irish chronicle this is what happened next:

First the Vikings constructed a roof of shields to put over their heads to protect themselves while they made a hole in the walls. What the Saxons and the Irish who were among them did was to hurl down huge boulders so that they crushed the shields on their heads. What the Vikings did to prevent this was to put great columns under the shields. What the Saxons did was to put the ale and water they found in the town into the town's cauldrons and boil it and throw it over the Vikings so that their skin peeled off them. The Vikings' response to that was to spread hides on top of the shields. The Saxons then scattered all the beehives that were in the town on top of the besiegers which prevented them from moving their hands and feet because of the number of bees stinging them. Not surprisingly, having seen their comrades crushed, boiled or stung to death, the Vikings gave up and went away.

Chester Burh

To 'Wodensfelt' (3 miles)

River Trent and the Danelaw (15 miles)

Tettenhall

Wooded slopes where the Mercian army could conceal themselves and ambush the Viking army

To Bridgnorth and the River Severn (12 miles)

Compton

Smestow Brook

To Wolverhampton

Wightwick

Pinch points where the valley narrows. The road could easily be blocked to trap the Viking army

Credit: Author

St Oswald and the Battle of Tettenhall

As a Christian, Aethelflaed was very fond of Anglo-Saxon saints. Her favourite was Oswald, who was King of Northumbria. He was one of the first Anglo-Saxons to convert to Christianity, but on August 5th 642 he was killed in battle, ironically by the pagan Mercian king, Penda. In 909 Oswald's bones lay deep in Danelaw territory when an Anglo-Saxon army went on a raid to retrieve them. The raid was successful and St Oswald's remains were brought back to Mercia and re-buried at Gloucester.

THE BATTLE OF TETTENHALL/ WEDNESFIELD

Perhaps the Danes were annoyed at Anglo-Saxons daring to raid their territory or perhaps they were just doing what Vikings do, either way in 910 a large Viking army went on a raid across the River Severn, deep into Mercia. Returning from their raid the Danes crossed the Severn near Bridgnorth on their way back to the safety of the Danelaw.

At the time, Aethelflaed's brother, Edward, who was by now King of Wessex, was in Kent waiting for his army on board ships sailing towards him. He was on the lookout for Viking raiders along the south coast of Wessex. It was unlikely he could be much help to his sister. But Aetheflaed had learnt well from her father. To defeat this army Aethelflaed needed to raise a large army as quickly as possible. Wednesfield, or Woden's Heath in Anglo-Saxon, would have been the perfect place to meet. It was half way between Bridgnorth and the Danelaw and at a cross roads of important tracks going East-West and North-South. Furthermore Woden was still a legendary Anglo-Saxon war hero; he had been worshipped as a god until the Anglo-Saxons converted to Christianity. By meeting at Woden's Heath, they must have felt their great hero was looking over them to ensure their success. But if it was the best place to gather, it would not have been the best place to attack a Viking army almost certainly on horseback. The Vikings valued horses as much as they valued their ships since it gave them speed of movement. Important Viking leaders have been found buried with their horses.

Anglo-Saxon Pillar at St Peter's Church, Wolverhampton

THE BATTLE OF TETTENHALL/ WEDNESFIELD

The perfect place to attack, however, was only 3 or 4 miles away near Tettenhall where the Smestow Valley narrows. Here they could hide in the wooded slopes before unleashing a hail of spears and arrows on the unsuspecting Vikings. The date of the battle is recorded as August 5th, St Oswald's day. For Aethelflaed this was an important day and she must have thought that her favourite Christian saint was also looking over her.

No one can be sure exactly what happened, but if the Vikings, on their horses, were driven into the marshes of the Smestow Valley, they would have become an easy target. Since Viking leaders also wore armour, this would also explain why we are told so many kings were killed at Tettenhall. It is very hard to swim in a suit of armour!

Smestow Valley with information plaque

AFTER TETTENHALL

In 911 her husband, Aethelred, died and was buried at St Oswald's Priory in Gloucester. As it was the custom in Wessex that no woman could take the title of queen, Aethelflaed never called herself the Queen of the Mercians. In Wales, however, she was known as the Queen of the Mercians and one chronicler even calls her a greater leader than Caesar.

With so many Viking leaders killed, Aethelflaed began taking back territory from the Danes and building even more burhs, including Tamworth, an ancient Anglo-Saxon capital. In many cases the Danes submitted without a fight, but one Danish stronghold was determined to resist: this was Derby. In 917, however, the town was finally taken though not without some personal grief for Aethelflaed as 'four of her thegns who were most dear to her, were killed there inside the gates'.

A year later the great Viking city of York also submitted to Aethelflaed without a fight and so, with the help of her brother Edward, she had created one Anglo-Saxon Kingdom. Sadly, just a few days later, Aethelflaed died suddenly at Tamworth. Her body was taken to Gloucester where she was buried next to her husband in accordance with her wishes.

Soon after, Edward took Aethelflaed's daughter, Aelfwynn, and led her away to Wessex where she probably ended up in a nunnery. He now saw himself as the ruler of Wessex and Mercia.

Oswald's Priory Gloucester

ATHELSTAN

Athelstan was just six years old when Edward placed him in the care of his sister, Aethelflaed. It is not known why, but Edward had re-married and the family of his second wife would have been keen for her children to succeed Edward as King of Wessex. This could have put Athelstan in some danger.

When Edward died in 924, the Mercians immediately proclaimed Athelstan as their king. This did not go down too well in Wessex. They wanted Edward's other son, Aelfweard, to be crowned as King of all the Anglo-Saxons. But just two weeks after his father's death, Aelfweard also died.

The son of Edward, but brought up by his aunt in Mercia, Aethelstan was now the perfect choice to unite the ancient kingdoms of Wessex and Mercia into one kingdom – England. He chose to be crowned at Kingston on Thames, on the border between Wessex and Mercia, as a way of showing that the ancient kingdoms were now united.

Athelstan was not only the first King of England, but in learning lessons from his aunt, he went on to become one of England's greatest rulers. That, however, is another story.

The Tomb of King Athelstan in Malmesbury Abbey

DID YOU KNOW?

- When Tolkein wrote his famous book, The Lord of the Rings, he based Arwen, the Elf Queen, on Aethelflaed.

- The gates at the former Wolverhampton Environment Centre, in the Smestow Valley were designed by Tolkien Brothers, relatives of the author.

- Most of our everyday words, such as the parts of our body, are from the Anglo-Saxons. Toe, finger and foot are all Anglo Saxon, though skull and skin, like most words beginning 'sk' are Viking words (Old Norse).

- There are many words in English which come from the Vikings, though some have changed their meaning. Cloud used to mean a rocky hill top (in parts of Staffordshire and Derbyshire there are still hills called clouds such as Hen Cloud). The Viking word for cloud was sky!

- The days of the week are named after Anglo-Saxon and Viking pagan gods.

- The name Starbucks can be traced back to a Viking family who settled in Yorkshire. They lived near a stream where sedges grew. The Viking name for sedge was star and a stream was called a beck so they were called the Starbeck family. When, many years later, some of the family moved to America their name changed to Starbuck. Starbuck is a well-known character in the American novel 'Moby Dick'. That is why a group of American students chose to call their coffee chain 'Starbucks'. There is, however, still a place near Harrogate in Yorkshire called Starbeck.

- Place names ending in 'ton' or 'ham', meaning a settlement, are Anglo-Saxon. Place names ending 'by' or 'thorpe' are Viking. There are no place names ending in 'by' or 'thorpe' west of the old Danelaw.

Hen Cloud

HOW DO WE KNOW

The Primary Sources

The main source of information is the Anglo-Saxon Chronicles. These were initiated by Alfred the Great as a history of the Anglo-Saxon people and written in the Anglo-Saxon language. After his death, copies of the chronicles were distributed to various monasteries where they were kept up to a greater or lesser extent. It is the Abingdon manuscript which gives us most of our information about Aethelflaed and is referred to as the Mercian register. The other manuscripts conspicuously avoid mentioning Aethelflaed until her death in 918, but it should be noted that these manuscripts originated in Wessex and highlight the Wessex dynasty. They were also written in monasteries where the role of a woman as a warrior leader would have been met with considerable disapproval – particularly in Wessex. The chronicles agree, however, that the Vikings were defeated at Tettenhall. The relevant quotes for the year 910 are as follows:

The Winchester Chronicle

Here the raiding army in Northumbria broke the peace, and scorned every peace which King Edward and his councillors offered them and raided across the land of Mercia. And the King was then in Kent and the ships went east along the south coast towards him. Then the raiding army imagined that the most part of his reinforcement was on these ships, and that they may go unfought wherever they wanted. Then when the King learnt that they had gone out on a raid, he sent his army both from Wessex and Mercia and they got in front of the raiding army from behind when it was on its way home and then fought with them and put the raiding army to flight, and killed many thousands of it; and King Eowils was killed there.

Aethelflaed statue at Runcorn

The Abingdon Manuscript (The Mercian Register)

In this year the English and the Danes fought at Tettenhall and the English took the victory. In the same year Aethelflaed built the stronghold at Bremesbyrig (location uncertain).

The Worcester Manuscript

This version mentions the battle twice – once for the year 909 and then again for 910.
909: Here the Mercians and West Saxons fought against the raiding army near Tettenhall on 6 August and had the victory. And the same year Aethelflaed built Bremesburh.

910: Here the English and the Danes fought at Tettenhall, and Aethelred, leader of the Mercians passed away.

The Peterborough Manuscript

Here the English raiding army and the Danes fought at Tettenhall, and Aethelred, leader of the Mercians passed away.
(The slight variations in these accounts would suggest that they are not mere copies.)
Another chronicler is Aethelweard. He was writing about 980. He was also from Wessex and related to Edward the Elder. He was asked to write a history of the Anglo-Saxon people for another relative who was an abbess on the continent.

Aethelflaed and Athelstan statue at Tamworth